P9-DVU-441

MISFITS

MISFITS

A Personal Manifesto

MICHAELA COEL

Henry Holt and Company Ⓗ New York

Henry Holt and Company
Publishers since 1866
120 Broadway
New York, New York 10271
www.henryholt.com

Henry Holt® and **Ⓗ**® are registered trademarks of Macmillan
Publishing Group, LLC.

Copyright © 2021 by Michaela Coel
All rights reserved.
Distributed in Canada by Raincoast Book Distribution
Limited

An earlier abridged version of this text was first presented at
the Edinburgh International Television Festival as a James
MacTaggart Memorial Lecture given in the United Kingdom,
in 2018.

Quote on p. 95 extracted from *Act Accordingly* by Colin Wright
(2013) and reproduced with permission from the author.

Library of Congress Cataloging-in-Publication data is
available.

ISBN 9781250843449

Our books may be purchased in bulk for promotional,
educational, or business use. Please contact your local
bookseller or the Macmillan Corporate and Premium Sales
Department at (800) 221-7945, extension 5442, or by e-mail
at MacmillanSpecialMarkets@macmillan.com.

First U.S. Edition 2021

Published in the United Kingdom by Ebury Publishing. Ebury
Publishing is part of the Penguin Random House group of
companies.

Designed by Meryl Sussman Levavi

Moth artwork by Alexis Eke

Printed in the United States of America

10 9 8 7 6 5 4 3 2 1

To the one who always
gets me out of trouble,
Jasmine Aboagye,
and the Mama who
born'd us.

Ode on Melancholy

JOHN KEATS

No, no, go not to Lethe, neither twist
 Wolf's-bane, tight-rooted, for its poisonous wine;
Nor suffer thy pale forehead to be kiss'd
 By nightshade, ruby grape of Proserpine;
  Make not your rosary of yew-berries,
 Nor let the beetle, nor the death-moth be
  Your mournful Psyche, nor the downy owl
A partner in your sorrow's mysteries;
 For shade to shade will come too drowsily,
  And drown the wakeful anguish of the soul.

But when the melancholy fit shall fall
 Sudden from heaven like a weeping cloud,
That fosters the droop-headed flowers all,
 And hides the green hill in an April shroud;
Then glut thy sorrow on a morning rose,
 Or on the rainbow of the salt sand-wave,
  Or on the wealth of globed peonies;
Or if thy mistress some rich anger shows,
 Emprison her soft hand, and let her rave,
  And feed deep, deep upon her peerless eyes.

She dwells with Beauty—Beauty that must die;
 And Joy, whose hand is ever at his lips
Bidding adieu; and aching Pleasure nigh,
 Turning to poison while the bee-mouth sips:
Ay, in the very temple of Delight
 Veil'd Melancholy has her sovran shrine,
     Though seen of none save him whose strenuous
tongue
 Can burst Joy's grape against his palate fine;
His soul shalt taste the sadness of her might,
     And be among her cloudy trophies hung.

Contents

MISFITS

INTRODUCTION

Hello,

Thank you so much for picking up this book and peeling back the first page to discover its contents.

I will do what I'm best at: tell stories, in the hope that you'll be able to connect the dots, find threads to tie together.

I like TV, I like making burritos and I like my friends, so sometimes I combine all three by inviting friends over to make burritos and watch telly on my projector. One night back in 2018, my friends complained that the smell of the onions I was chopping was too strong and opened up the window. Cue a moth now dancing around the projector light, interrupting the visual perfection of *Stranger Things*. Moths disturb me, my peace and my flow, with their incessant fluttering. Their erratic, unpredictable movements get me the hell anxious—I hate them. I've always hated them, so of course I have moth-killer spray on hand. I spray the ray of light until the moth is dead on the floor. I'm so scared of 'em I can't even bear to deal with their dead bodies, so I ask my friend to pick up the corpse with some kitchen paper and dispose of it. But that friend is busy coughing—in fact, all my friends are now coughing, covering their noses and mouths, burying their faces in my sofa or their clothes. I've sprayed too much, apparently. The smell is insufferable.

I, however, am not bothered by the moth spray, just as I wasn't bothered by the scent of onions. The flat descends into chaos as my friends alternate between hanging their heads out of the window for air or running out of my flat entirely. I stand as still as the moth's corpse. I inhale: my nasal pathways are clear. I walk around and begin sniffing things in the flat, curiously burrowing my nose inside shoes, coffee beans, vinegar, my coughing housemate's armpits. I feel and hear the air traveling smoothly into my nasal passages, but that journey has no scent accompanying it.

Later, I seek medical help. The doctors don't know why this has happened, but they say they've seen the sense of smell return after two or three years. I am offered smell training, a method known for successfully awakening the olfactory nerves. I refuse.

Of all the senses to lose, smell is not one I minded severing my relationship with. In fact, had I not sprayed moth-killer that day and seen my friends freak out, how long would I have carried on, oblivious to the fact that my ability to smell was gone? How long had I already lived oblivious to the fact that it had gone? I'd go so far as to say I like having anosmia.

Yes, I cannot smell smoke in the event of a fire anymore, and expiration dates on food items are something to worship rather than to test one's fate on, but losing one sense enabled me to enhance my use of the others; listening, looking and feeling everything and everyone around me with more attention than before. No more smelling sewage pipes, cat piss, the stench of fish from the local monger—nothing fishy will ever be going on again. Sweet.

Here I am in a public toilet cubicle, staring into the mouth of the bowl as one stares into the soul of a Gustavo Nazareno piece at a gallery . . . someone else's unflushed feces slumbers in the water, thick skid marks marring porcelain . . . I can't smell anything, and so I guess everything smells just fine.

That same year, 2018, I am asked to write and present a lecture to professionals within the television industry. The invitation comes as I am wrapping up on playing Kate Ashby in Hugo Blick's *Black Earth Rising*. At the time I've never heard of the MacTaggart Lecture. Then again, back then, I'd also never heard of Depeche Mode or Sarajevo, so no shade to the lecture—it just hadn't beamed onto my radar. The MacTaggart Lecture is an annual event that takes place at the Edinburgh TV Festival in front of an audience of four thousand. I have no idea what I might write about or whether I am truly qualified to offer a lecture to anyone, and find the idea of speaking behind a podium for an hour to be very unattractive. However, I am told this sort of opportunity isn't the kind you turn down, so with naïveté and palpitations, I accept.

I begin in leafy Somerset, in a house generously lent to me by my drama commissioner: a "space to think and write" type of thing. It's an old house, stationed near a post office and not much else. Built on the grounds of what used to be a chapel. In the verdant garden, the chapel still sits.

I unpack my bags and for days, write tirelessly. Eventually I come up with a first draft, funny in some places, brutally honest, concluding with a positive message about the joy and purpose creating stories has given to my life. *It's good,* I think; *it's fine.*

I finally allow my back to lean against the sofa, and as the afternoon sun flirts with my eyelids, I fall asleep.

I enter a dream.

The dream goes like this: I'm in the exact same position on the sofa, stirring awake instead of falling asleep, and it's the dead of night. A group of men have found their way into the house and are taking novelty selfies with my sleeping body in the background. As soon as they notice I'm awake, they apologize and sprint out of the house.

I chase them, shouting, "Don't worry about the pictures, it's okay—I actually need help."

They look at each other nervously.

I tell them I am trying to leave the house they found me in, that I'd like to book an Uber from my phone, but that for some reason I can't see the screen. I ask if one of them could take my phone and book it for me.

After some mild hesitation, one of the men takes my phone. Now that I can see them up close, I notice how diverse they are, in height, skin tone, age. I inspect the seven-foot-something White man in a kente ball gown.

"I like your dress," I say.

Both of his cheeks beam a glowing red. He grins and appears so overwhelmed with joy that his eyes water.

"Thank you," he says.

One of the men hands me back my phone, having successfully called an Uber. I thank the men, and we say goodbye. I sit on a bench outside the house and wait. The night sky is freckled with stars, a vision both arresting and sedating. Strange-colored shapes seem to shoot across the sky. It's terrifying, my heart races, but I try to be calm. *Whatever that is is far away in the night sky, and it can't hurt you,* I think to myself. I begin to wonder why I wanted to leave such a lovely place, and as I decide that I want to stay, two pickup trucks arrive. A chirpy woman hops out of one, a chirpy man hops out of the other.

Woman: "Uber?"

Man: "Did somebody call for an Uber?"

My heart sinks. I explain to them that one of the strangers must have booked from their own phone as well as on mine, which has resulted in two drivers and one passenger. Oops. Not only that, but I no longer want to leave. Now their hearts sink.

"Oh, we don't get many calls round here," says the woman.

The guilt leads me down an internal rabbit hole of problem-solving.

Plan A: I will be able to get into both Ubers if I split myself in two. Scientifically, this is certain death: they'll both have half a dead Michaela in their vehicles, and the publicity storm arising from this will ensure they'll never work again.

They wait with patient contentment as I think frantically.

Plan B: I *could* ride in both Ubers if every mile I jump out and switch vehicles. On the other hand, that is a lot of stopping and starting for them, and on the highways they'd ideally want to cruise the journey without extra interference.

My "aha!" moment comes: I look to the woman and make a proposition.

"Leave your truck here, you and I will get into this gentleman's vehicle, and he'll drive us to London, he'll drive you back, you pick up your truck, and then the both of you can split the fee."

Immediately they respond, "Great, that works."

I get inside. I sit in front, beside the man, and the woman sits in the back. We zoom happily down country roads. I look down at the floor, where my feet are placed, and realize it goes much deeper than a standard vehicle's. There is a large black dog under there, roaming back and forth from the gentleman's side of the vehicle, where the clutch, brake and gas are, to mine: across and back, across and back, slowly, trance-like. I am surprised.

"There's a dog."

The driver responds, with the gentle tenderness he has embodied throughout, "Yes, are you scared?"

"No, I just didn't know it was there." We continue the journey in silence. Until . . .

A flutter.

Now there's a moth. The three of us try to swat it away as the pink of dawn ascends.

I like to search for meaning in the meaningless, so I afterward recount the dream to friends, family and colleagues to see what they think.

"The house is the business," many say. I like that. "The Uber drivers represent the producers," say others. I like that, too: I question why, in the dream, I deferred to a man to drive, and why the woman was so willing to get in the back, going from driver to passenger to get half of the fee. Someone else said a black dog in a dream is normally symbolic of a guide. But if it was my guide I wondered why it was mindlessly attempting to travel east to west while trapped in a vehicle that was journeying southward. No one could take a stab at what the moth itself was until I asked a colleague, who said: "I think the moth represents your spirit, that doesn't want to be a part of any of this."

I am moved to tears. Perhaps some unconscious part of me identifies with this interpretation, but also I'm a millennial: we love a spirit animal.

There are an estimated 140,000 to 160,000 identified species of moths, and an estimated 560,000 more which are yet to be described and labeled. Although some are active during the day (diurnal), and others during twilight (crepuscular), moths are predominantly nocturnal creatures, preferring to be active in the dark, pollinating flowers at night just as butterflies typically do during daylight. Considering this preference to roam in darkness, it's surprising that moths find themselves circling around the very thing they typically avoid: light (this phenomenon is known as positive phototaxis), and the reason for this is a scientific mystery. Some scientists believe it is because the brightness interferes with their navigational system, so the light source seems more distant than it really is.

Moths don't have noses to smell through, and yet they are expert sniffers, with sense receptors (sensilla) scattered over their antennae, palps, legs, proboscis or other parts of the body; female moths specifically can detect chemicals through their abdominal tip.

In various cultures around the world, moths are often seen as a bad omen. In Mexico, the Black Witch moth (*la mariposa de la muerte*) is considered a carrier of bad news, flying through windows to collect the souls of those on their deathbeds. The name Mayan people gave this moth reflects its frequent flutter into people's homes: "Ma-Ha-Nah," which means "may I borrow your house?"

In Jamaica they're known as "duppy bats" and embody lost souls.

Moths seem to play an interesting role in Irish folklore, too. An old Irish expression for crushing a person: *"na féileacán a bhrú as duine"* means to push the butterfly—or soul—out of someone. In Latin American countries, part of the Saturniidae family of moths is highly toxic and the cause of a number of casualties every year.

The notion of the moth as a symbol of death is partly attributed to three moth species of the genus *Acherontia*, found throughout Africa, Asia and Europe; the pattern of markings on the back of one of these moths is human skull-shaped, and because of this they are nicknamed the "death's-head hawkmoth."

As well as being the only moth sexy enough to pose for the artwork of *The Silence of the Lambs*, the death's-head hawkmoth is one of the few of its species that can, believe it or not, use their pharynx to create sound. Many moths survive on a diet of nectar, a sweet liquid made by flowers, which they suck through a tube called a proboscis. The death's-head hawkmoth is the only moth that has evolved its sucking technique to allow thicker liquid to flow freely, and this is because it doesn't survive on nectar, but on honey. This modification to its pharynx caused further tweaks like making sound possible, and necessary as, to get honey, the hawkmoth has to enter the hives of honey bees. When hungry predators advance toward them they inflate and deflate a chamber in their heads to produce a squeak, higher in pitch than a cicada and just as harmless. This little sound is about the only defense mechanism the death's-head hawkmoth has, despite the terror its name induces.

As the weeks progress, I dig a little deeper into my unconscious and try to reflect on my life and career with an enhanced sense. The tone of my lecture begins to morph. I read previous drafts and deem them fragile, naive, exposing. How am I able to be so transparent on paper about rape, malpractice and poverty, yet still compartmentalize? It's as though I were telling the truth while simultaneously running away from it.

The positive finish of the lecture begins to gross me out. Things are not fine now; the shit I could recount so easily is not fine, it is shit, and it stinks. If I am going to offer it on a silver platter to others, I had best try to get a sense of what it smells like. Although the details of the lecture remain the same, my sense of the details begins to change: I sense my pain, brokenness, fragility. It's as if I'd always known my house was on fire, but I am suddenly smelling the smoke.

What I am writing doesn't change, but *how* I write it changes drastically. I find myself sitting with pain, with darkness. "How long," I begin to wonder, "has my habit been to recount horror with a smile, standing in the light recalling tales of darkness?" Long enough that being here, with this darkness, feels foreign.

As I redraft, I take myself back to that darkness, to that sensation of pain, and sit with it. It is terrifying; my heart races. I tell myself to be calm: it is far away and can't hurt me. Considering my initial revulsion, the mysteries of the moth slowly lure me in, eventually offering me reassurance. My perception of the moth changes, and while remaining honest, my speech transmogrifies into a mystery. I am choosing language that lacks transparency, choosing to remain on this bench, in the dark, and inviting each listener to meet me here instead. I redraft with this sense, and I keep rewriting until I am told I must stop. I never really finish the lecture—does anything ever finish? My things are thrown back in the bag they came in; I sign the house guestbook with a no doubt peculiar allusion to a moth, and say goodbye to lovesome Somerset.

Back in London, my housemate, Ash, helps me drill down into the lecture. I am overwhelmed, emotional, erratic, nervous. He is coaching me, forcing me to repeat the sentences until I can get through them without crying.

In the days before the lecture I take a leisurely browse through the handmade goods of various jewelry makers on Etsy and order myself a death's-head hawkmoth necklace.

Then the day comes. I am in Scotland, standing in front of a bright artificial light with a microphone pointed at my mouth. The necklace of the moth is hidden beneath my dress, and Ash is sitting beside my cousin, Joel, in the auditorium. The seats are full; people sit on the stairs and stand behind the back row. It is indeed terrifying. My heart races.

My brain slows down, circles away from the hazardous stars, away from the frantic movement of unfamiliar shapes, until it eventually descends into the dark, hovering onto the bench, a calmer place from which to think, and I open my mouth to speak.

MISFITS

*A Personal
Manifesto*

Somehow, I find myself standing before every-one, in front of a podium, to give a "lecture." Ex-boyfriends have accused me of giving these, uni-versities have accused me of never attending them, but my relationship with this word has a rebirth: the MacTaggart Lecture. Let's face it, though, I don't really know how it works in this house yet. Unlike my wonderful predecessor, broadcaster Jon Snow, this whole "reading things I haven't memorized from a screen for strangers" thing is brand-new shit, but I'm so, so glad for this opportunity, this platform, and for the urgency it's instilled in me to learn, but I'm also really nervous. Who wouldn't be nervous? Maybe only like, 5 percent? Ninety-five percent of most people in any room would be a rack of nerves. It's a bit much, innit?

I am thankful for having been invited to speak as a creative to you—to producers; to broadcasters; to those aspiring for careers in such fields. As a creative,

I decide I'm going to do what I do best: I'm going to tell you all a story. Maybe you can look for patterns.

I was born and raised in London. The Square Mile, sometimes considered Tower Hamlets, sometimes considered "City of London"; home to both the Stock Exchange and the Bank of England.

Between its modern corporate skyscraper towers and medieval alleyways exists a social housing estate. Right there, in plain sight, yet somehow unseen. It was originally built in 1977, with the aim to help homeless people in London, and that's my proud home. Even now, there may be someone rushing past it for the hundredth time, briefcase in hand, with no idea this council estate exists.

We lived directly opposite the Royal Bank of Scotland, which somehow felt "other" and slightly bizarre. Not the Scottish bit, the Royal Bank bit.

At most, we, being my mother, sister and I, were one of four Black families there. Not something I thought anyone gave a damn about, until someone left a pile of shit on our doorstep. My mum silently cleaned it up. But when we received a bag of shit through our letterbox, as a precocious busybody I felt I had no choice but to take things into my seven-year-old hands. I walked around the estate, swung on the swings, desperate for transparency, wondering, *Who? . . . Who are the enemies of my family?*

I figured it was Sam, so I'd call her an ugly wanker, then Sam would call me a dirty nigger. We would fight. That was just our way of expressing our mistrust and fear of those who were visually or

That was just our way of expressing

our mistrust and fear of those who

were visually or culturally different

from us.

culturally different from us. But we also had fun. The same Sam would be at mine for Nintendo between scraps; my mum would make us scones.

The miracle of my estate was Willy. On the best of days, he'd lean out of his window and sprinkle halal penny sweets down. As they fell, every child of every color and creed would scramble from the playground and scrabble for a sweet.

These sweets weren't wrapped or nothing; the tastebuds were fully aware of the pavement in the mix, but we didn't mind. The point was you got a sweet today and other people didn't. Are you chewing? "Iss lit." You're lit.

Not far from the Square Mile there's a theatre, where you might say my route into TV started.

Mother, a single, hardworking immigrant to England, was a health and social sciences student and a weekend cleaner. She discovered a theatre would allow children from low-income families to join their youth workshops—for free. Free was cheaper than childcare, and at eight years old I was a part of Bridewell Youth Theatre. The only Black person.

I loved it; we played from morning till noon, and we'd sometimes even appear as ensemble in their main plays. I didn't know or care what the plays were about, but I would cry for weeks when they ended, 'cause it meant a cast were leaving that had just started to feel like family.

Later I joined a girls' secondary school in my borough, where new bonds replaced lost ones. A crew of ten misfits, mainly hailing from Africa and the Caribbean. I'll never forget our first IT class, pretending to listen to a teacher ramble on about modems and CD-ROMs, then the sudden sound of glass shattering out of what was a window, just seconds before a girl's head was smashed through it. Even more disturbing was the sound in the room that immediately followed: laughter.

We eleven-year-olds learned the rules of the game quickly; from nine to three, laugh or be laughed at, and after three? Go home, to your room, and cry, while in my case attaching my head-brace.

This was a Catholic school in which student prostitution wasn't a shock, but a gorgeous bit of gossip to spread. A school in which you could, on weekends, find the rare sighting of a teacher in the middle of an East London market slouched on a curb on the cusp of alcohol-induced paralysis; and as one would a shooting star, you were lucky if you caught a glimpse.

This was the 2000s. We were the generation of twelve-year-olds with Nokia 3310s. The One2One network would malfunction and calls would unintentionally be free. That's right, *free calls!* The news would fly like falcons through our communities—and upon the wings of those eastward falcons? The most important of news: Janette sucked her own left tit; Clare had sex at the back of the bus with Bola; Martina's selling bagels out of a bin bag for 20p—25p if you want ketchup.

By 2002, though, our perception of IT was taking a strange turn. This wasn't a boring waste of time, this was a training ground for the most powerful weapon a girl of thirteen could have: the anonymous creation of webpages. What faster, cheaper way to disseminate, implicate and destroy? A new age had begun: a sharper knife, a silent gun with limitless bullets, trigger puller unknown; delicious, until I found myself on the wrong end of it, as the "big-lipped coconut who gave three blow jobs last week."

A coconut: an insult used to describe one who is Black on the outside but White on the inside, as you would imagine a coconut. Or you could just imagine looking at the first Black girl in the school's history to join in the Irish dance team— that's what I was. I performed, middle of the row, fuckin' smashed it.

But blow jobs? I was outraged. The only thing I was blowing was the clarinet. I'd been bullied about these lips for a while. As I'd fine-tuned my clarinet skills, alone in the music room, some of the older girls in my school would come in and block the door. They'd insult my lips, how big they were, how ugly they were, releasing me only when the tears became visible. Needless to say . . . I had a sturdy amount of baggage, that fueled me . . . into creating my first-ever webpage.

A coconut: an insult used to describe

one who is Black on the outside but

White on the inside, as you would

imagine a coconut.

Although those sites were anonymous, I decided to sacrifice my anonymity by mentioning those unique insults thrown my way. What I threw back was an attack, not on them, but on their ideals. "Imma geek, so what?" "My trainers ain't designer, so what?" "I love the Irish step dance, so what?" I made it funny. I insulted myself. But also let it be known, I didn't give a fuck.

One day, the Queen sat next to me in science. And she really was considered by all of us a real Queen, like Claire Foy.* Soft, gentle, easily recognizable by her loud, brash laugh. I'd never spoken to her, hadn't dared. I just felt this intrinsic desire to respect and keep distance. But she sat there, looked me in the eye and whispered she was pregnant and breaking the news to me in advance so I'd keep her off my webpage. She let me feel her baby bump, the first I'd ever felt, in her fourteen-year-old belly; a baby having a baby. The webpages were brutal; printouts would pass around classes; we'd giggle at public destruction, the occasional laugh-snort marred with mania and misery heard. I respected her more than anyone I'd ever met, but even if I hadn't, even if I'd hated her, I'd no desire to put that information anywhere. May her soul rest in peace.

One time, I was passing my main bully in the corridor, one of the older ones that would lock me in the music room. She was on the phone, roaming back and forth, stressed; nonetheless she had a few seconds for me: "Look at your fat lip." I turned to her, and agreed. I added that it was the hardest part of my mum's pregnancy—pushing them out. I said she seemed stressed and asked if she wanted a hug. She never spoke to me again.

Coming from the tiny Square Mile, and a tiny family, what carried me through those five years was the abundance of Black girls, White girls, mixed girls, misfits; my friends were all misfits: a huge gang of commercially unattractive, beautiful misfits, who found the mainstream world unattractive. From the outside we were difficult to distinguish, but on the inside known by name, and nature. Marisa: her nickname was Mash and we would pretend to be twins. Trecia: nickname Trash, short, but with a roster of jokes and undercuts so tall she would always feel secure of her place as an equal within the squad. Both Ghanaian, both from Hackney. Nichaela—yup, my name but with an "N," and like our names, we were similar but different: she had natural hair, but longer; she had chocolate skin, but it spread itself over a longer body; she loved talking about vaginas, but unlike me drew the line at showing each other our period pads. Shakira (Shax for short): Guyanese, wore a red coat and carried a red umbrella to school every day, yes, even on dry days. Kate (Kath, sometimes Kathapilla, Kathical): White girl from round the way

Coming from the tiny Square Mile, and a tiny family, what carried me through those five years was the abundance of Black girls, White girls, mixed girls, misfits; my friends were all misfits: a huge gang of commercially unattractive, beautiful misfits, who found the mainstream world unattractive. From the outside we were difficult to distinguish, but on the inside known by name, and nature.

(back then we didn't think to ask White people that shit; in fact, at the time of writing, origins still unknown), mouthy, and far more cynical than any twelve-year-old should be. Amy: braces, eerily quiet, happiest when in the company of girls and girls alone; the one the boys chased every time we went bowling or to Trocadero; the one that made me understand in my soul that being seen as pretty by the young boys of the day was as stressful as not being seen by them at all. Bianca, Joanna, Jenine, Rochelle, Maame. Within the group there was a girl band, Black Voices Inc. We wrote our own lyrics, the topics of which were usually boys we'd encountered on the bus. Or the fact that the school was so shitty the heaters were literally falling off the walls. My friend Celestina would sing: "Plastic roof, falling heaters, they think we're Barbie and Ken."

This isn't only what carried me through those years—those girls made those the best five of my life. New bonds replaced lost ones upon finding myself in a church. I fell in love with God. With Jesus. His actions, his character. I read the Bible and loved its metaphors, its hope. It's what propelled me into becoming a poet.

It was clear I liked telling stories. I was told to apply for something called a drama school, so I dropped out of uni, again. It was my second go at it, and in two years I'd been to only one English lecture. The lecture was fine, was good, but I bumped into a friend on the way out and found out I'd just sat through a lecture for law students. I'd no idea. I'd even taken notes. So I left, to "tell stories." My mum was concerned; she was an NHS mental health nurse at the time, and what could she do but watch my future fall into uncertainty?

Where was I climbing to? Why was there no clear sign of safety at the end of the ladder?

I got in, to a drama school. In a year of only twenty-three. A drama school in my Square Mile; I'd grown up walking past it my whole life not knowing what it was, and now I was a member of its family. I was told its theatre attracted agents from far and wide, and during the final year they'd come to see us perform and sign the hottest talent. Like kids scrabbling for a sweet from above. Silk Street Theatre—where the hottest talent met the hottest agents, to partner with the hottest casting directors, to make the hottest period dramas.

I was the first Black girl they'd accepted in five years, a fact which the head of the school described to me as "the elephant in the room." This was my third attempt at a university. I'd still never been into a pub, to a festival. I just hadn't. I'd never watched *Fawlty Towers* or *Red Dwarf* or heard of any festival in Edinburgh, I just hadn't, and struggled to converse on things I didn't know about. I was watching a lot of TV—*Seinfeld, Moesha, The Golden Girls, Buffy*—shows no one really spoke about. So, I spent most of my time perched in the corridor, hoodie up.

I was called a nigger twice in drama school. The first was by a teacher during a "walk in the space" improvisation that had nothing to do with race. "Oi, nigger, what you got for me?" We students continued walking in the space, the two Black boys and I glancing at each other whenever we passed . . . "Who's she talking to?" we'd whisper, "Boy, not me," "Nah, that was for you," passing around responsibility like a hot potato, muffling our laugh-snorts. I wonder what the other students thought of our complicity. The second time was a girl in my own year. After class, the same two boys and I found ourselves perched in the corridor; she passed and waved. "See you later, niggers!" . . . We three Blacks of Orient were posed with a dilemma—"niggers" . . . plural. This hot potato belonged to us all. I chose to act. I called her back and calmly gave her sound advice. She smiled, continued her way and never said sorry.

Drama school was problematic in so many ways. As an Evangelical Christian, the plan was to teach the homosexuals about Jesus, but I accidentally ended up becoming best friends with some and learning from these other kind of misfits. Yes, homosexual bonds replaced biblical ones. I still love the character of Jesus. I just started paying attention to the stuff written around Him, and didn't care for what I read.

We were told at school, if we wanted to pursue this, we should be "yes" people, and expect to be poor for the rest of our lives. "Climb because you want to tell stories." I loved the concept! All of us united, climbing toward storytelling at the risk of poverty, screaming "Yes!"

In a class exercise, however, the teacher commanded we run to point A if our parents owned a home or to point B if they didn't. When everybody else ran to point A, and I found myself isolated at point B, I was astounded. Had land-owning taken over my race? *Why did this class exercise even exist?* I thought, then blogged about it. Not about how hard it was not owning a house; I wrote about the resilience born from having no safety net at all, having to climb ladders with no stable ground beneath you.

On top of it, all our ladders were faulty, born climbing a ladder before we could walk, and better climb fast lest it snap beneath your feet! I told people to keep climbing, for the love of it, whatever the craft, not because of financial profit, or safety. What is "safety"? I wrote that such circumstances can leave you feeling destined for defeat, or it could do something else; it could breed a determination, a relentless pursuit of one's dreams that no safe man could ever replicate. I changed the narrative, twisting it in my favor.

This idea of a profit ladder was producing such a desperate pursuit in some around me. For those who had no means of getting more—they were arrested. I was aware, even then, that the proportion of Black people imprisoned in the UK was almost seven times our share of the population. *Seven* times.

I blogged again.

I wrote about the resilience born from having no safety net at all, having to climb ladders with no stable ground beneath you.

On top of it, all our ladders were faulty, born climbing a ladder before we could walk, and better climb fast lest it snap beneath your feet! I told people to keep climbing, for the love of it, whatever the craft, not because of financial profit, or safety.

What is "safety"?

One day an emergency meeting was scheduled between our year and the teachers. We gathered. Some students made small talk about the toilets not flushing, a teacher assured they'd be fixed, then BANG. "Michaela, what are these blogs?"

I'd upset people, people who didn't see color or class. A year later, a friend saw me perched in the corridor. She apologized for going to the teachers back then and orchestrating a meeting that she and many others knew would take place long before it occurred. I also knew that already, because a homosexual gave me a tip-off in advance: *tribe*.

I just loved the craft. I didn't mind the occasional "nigger" slip or military coup; I just wanted to be a lead on the Silk Street stage, I had to get a lead part at least once. I'm the first Black girl in half a decade! How could they *not*?

My ego's dreams came true. I was to play a role so important it was the name of the play— Lysistrata in *Lysistrata*—and my year were really happy for me. We only later found out this performance wouldn't be on Silk Street; it would be in South London, a thirty-five-minute drive across the river. My mates were sad. They hugged me. "No agent is going to come to this, Michaela, not the hot ones. They simply won't cross the river."

I lived in E1; everyone who lives in E1 knows: we live by the river, but even we don't cross it.

There was also the option to remove yourself from a main show to do a fifteen-minute solo piece; rarely did anyone do this as it wasn't on Silk Street, it was in the basement floor of the theatre.

But this wasn't about agents anymore; it was a chance to create something that wasn't a period drama designed in period costumes. I wanted to make something for this period, so I did both. I wrote a dark comedy called *Chewing Gum Dreams*. A title born from a poem; that poem born from an image in my mind. Of a tall council flat, tall as the Tower of Babel, winged falcons soaring round its highest floor in perpetual circles. Watching the jet planes and helicopters fly by, curious of life beyond their tower, but terrified of leaving it. Their wings were weighed down by gossip, dissemination, rivalry, fitting in, but also by love, passion, dreams. There's only so much a falcon could carry, so we'd offload the things society taught us were most superfluous: dreams, love and passion, and down they'd descend. Dreams, free-falling from our tower block, already forgotten before crashing into the pavement, trampled on by our newly acquired designer trainers, squashed into

I wanted to make something for this period, so I did both. I wrote a dark comedy called Chewing Gum Dreams. *A title born from a poem; that poem born from an image in my mind. Of a tall council flat, tall as the Tower of Babel, winged falcons soaring round its highest floor in perpetual circles. Watching the jet planes and helicopters fly by, curious of life beyond their tower, but terrified of leaving it.*

the pavement like chewing gum: *Chewing Gum Dreams*. I played eleven parts. The response in that basement was something neither I nor they had ever experienced, and on that high I did what I do best: I dropped out.

A graduate acquired land in Hackney; he'd turned it into a theatre, The Yard, and accepted my play for a four-day run despite my submission being late. Having read the script, he gave two notes; crucial notes. I listened. The rest, however—direction, set design, costume, flyer design, marketing—was down to me. I advertised on social media that if you met me in Tinsel Town, I'd buy you a milkshake if you bought a ticket. The milkshake brought a lot of people to the yard. I sat there from 1 p.m. till 1 a.m.; ticket sales increased. I did this while editing and rehearsing the script. It was exciting.

My show went up, and the audience went up with me, on my wings; responding, understanding, laughing and crying in every place I hoped they would. People came, who looked at things the way I did and saw they didn't fit; some felt they'd spent most of their lives being judged and disempowered before even speaking. The misfits were inspired—to create.

So I continued speaking. As an actor, at the National Theatre, I remained there for a year playing and bonding in various plays. I even had a four-day run of *Chewing Gum Dreams* at The Shed; a temporary theatre. It was great. Many more misfits came.

The play was read by a production company that sat under the umbrella of a huge production company. They asked if I wanted to make a TV show. "Yes of course holy shit yes."

They suggested I omit "Dreams" from the title. I said, "Yes of course holy shit sure." First, I was to write and read a twenty-minute version of what I imagined the TV show to look like and invite a small audience for a channel who were interested. I was then asked to write three five-minute scenes of TV to be uploaded onto the internet; those were the first attempts at scenes I'd ever written for TV. I had no practice; obviously, I was an outsider.

Yes, outsider. Not in a bad way, I wasn't out in the rain. I just wasn't here. When people mention "diversity" I can guess we mean people who aren't watching or making much of our telly, creatives "outside of" this industry. I can't use the word "diversity," because really I couldn't get clarity on it. I can't use "outsider" because the in/out thing becomes reminiscent of Brexit. So I'm gonna take

on another existing word—"misfit"—and change
the meaning of it just for this lecture.

I've already made my own website, with a dictio-
nary definition.

Here:

> **misfit**
> /'mɪs.fɪt/
> *noun*
> plural noun: **misfits**
>
> **The term "misfits" takes on dual notions; a
> misfit is one who looks at life differently.
> Many, however, are made into misfits
> because life looks at them differently; the
> UK's Black, Asian, and ginger communi-**

ties, for example. And there are many other examples.

The term "misfit" can be cross-generational and crosses concepts of gender or culture, simply by a desire for transparency, a desire to see another's point of view. Misfits who visibly fit in will sometimes find themselves merging with the mainstream, for a feeling of safety.

Synonyms: *outsider, falcon.*

I'm calling any challenge to my definition Fake News.

Of late, channels, production companies and online streaming services have found themselves scrabbling for misfits, like kids in a playground scrabbling for sweets, desperate for a chew. Not sure of the taste of these sweets, these dreams, just aware they might be very profitable.

The jet plane hovers over the tower, not sure where to land, how to land, if at all.

In the quest for new writers the misfit-looking people are instinctively sought after first. But instead of nurturing them to write for themselves, the last few years have seen an immediate coupling with writers before the process has begun. Writers more experienced, who fit into this house more.

Is it important that voices used to interruption get the experience of writing something without interference at least once?

We seem unsure, unknowing of their world and therefore their stories. So maybe we're a little tentative; uploading three or four short scenes; or one full episode, but online. The new creator uses social media platforms to tell their followers, the outsiders who don't watch telly, that finally they've been able to make something for TV—online.

The channel and producers study the comments on social media, investigating the audience's response. Is that important? I think so. In recent years, several major US shows have been canceled and revived by social media—such as *Brooklyn Nine-Nine*, *Sense8*, *Arrested Development* and *The Expanse*. This confirms that a medium outside of television is beginning to take control of it. Do you let them in, to start making it with you, or do you block them out? Does it matter?

Social media has done great things for us. It's allowed some of us to feel more loved, encouraged, connected, to make and share work, but it's also raised anxiety, paranoia and loneliness, in young people especially. Are we informing our young people of the possible negatives, or are we too busy capitalizing on it?

I don't know. I already told you I'm new to this house. But after the misfits enjoyed my three scenes, a producer called to say the head of the head of the head of the channel green-lit my series. The feeling of "yes" I liken to the standing ovation at the end of my play.

They asked me if I'd like to write the show alone. I said, "Yes of course holy shit sure yes." Patrons of the National Theatre who'd once heard me perform a poem asked if I was writing anything else. They gave me the keys to their second home, in America, by a lake; to write in, for no personal gain at all. I didn't realize just how disconnected this part of America would be, however.

Where were the people, the sirens, the noise? Where was the Wi-Fi? It was safe, so safe, too quiet. I'd check the doors were locked repeatedly, check social media perpetually. After a few days I had no choice but to relax. In those two weeks I wrote drafts of all six episodes. How had a falcon never flown to a lake?

Back in London my scripts were noted by the company. Notes were given on Friday nights and expected back redrafted by Monday. Calculating the hours easily, I saw I could reach my targets if I erased the concept of weekends, and saw sleeping as something you didn't do deeply, or every night, just some nights, like anal.

I still wasn't getting it right. The producer rang to say the commissioner thought I needed co-writers urgently. I got the call while shopping in Boots.* Standing in the aisle next to sanitary products, I was picking up some tights, then found myself sobbing into the tights, and discreetly leaving them there for someone else to buy.

I was making a story about the world from my view, from the view of those misfits I'd grown up

Calculating the hours easily, I saw

I could reach my targets if I erased

the concept of weekends, and saw

sleeping as something you didn't do

deeply, or every night,

just some nights, like anal.

with, who looked at things a bit like I did. A view rarely found on TV. Did these co-writers know my world from the inside? Or was their view vague? Could they distinguish our nature from the outside? I don't know, the exec producer pushed the head of comedy to read my scripts, after which the search for emergency co-writers was terminated.

For creatives, there is a beauty in carving your own story, conceiving it, at least once, alone, then allowing others to assist in nurturing and maturing it. Particularly for unheard voices, the voices denied, or for those who, given the opportunity to speak, find themselves surrendering to immediate interruption: Is co-writing immediate interruption? What would my scripts have been had they been interfered with at such an embryonic stage? I was relieved.

However, after draft 29, a friend discovered my body, on the floor, in the dark. I was looking for my brain. He asked what my script editor was doing. I asked what a script editor was. Whatever he told me, I got the sense that it was the TV equivalent of a doula.

I called the producers. They didn't want one, they wanted it to be my "baby." That's nice, but this is my first pregnancy; if we wanted this baby to be cute, instead of the newborn stroller the world wished it never peeked into, I couldn't do it alone and I needed a doctor.

"Things have to be episodic," said the script editor. I'd never heard that word before, "episodic." "And you haven't factored in commercial breaks. When you finish the first half, give them a reason to come back." He drew a map of my storylines on a whiteboard, and simply rearranged them, almost mathematically. I was impressed. He had great tools. He thought I had great stories. We began shooting.

I was on set all day, even when I wasn't in a scene. Doing rewrites in the trailer; assessing where I could save the producers money, despite having no clue how much that money was. I'd rewrite scenes so they could take place in the same location, returning scripts to them with clever cuts. I liked this feeling; I felt like they wanted me there. But this want became more of a need. A fine example is what came to be known as Trailer-Gate.

It was day one of the shoot. I approached the trailers to find five actors and actresses ranging in tones of brown and black, including the woman who plays my mother, bound up in one-third of a trailer. The second trailer was occupied by a White actress, looking like privileged piggy in the middle, and the third was mine—the writer's.

Prior to this I wouldn't have dared enter the production office, but I burst through the door. The room fell silent, like a scene in *EastEnders* and I was fully in Kat Slater* mode: "You know what that looks like, doncha? Like a fackin' slave ship!"

I know . . . I really did say that.

"I'm not racist!" a producer screamed at me. She was red with rage, wet with tears. "I know you ain't racist! That's what makes this all so fackin' bizarre!" I Kat Slatered the pub door behind me.

Hours passed. There was a line, myself and the actors on one side, the producers on the other, and it wasn't crossed, for hours. We were even shooting. The mood . . . was moody.

The executive producer came to me, the outsider to production, and asked, "What do we do?" I suggested he apologize to everyone, buy my on-screen mum some flowers and get more trailers. They did.

I asked the actors why they agreed to share. They just wanted it to work, their belief in the job only matched by their anxiety of losing it. I apologized. I told them we were working for a reputable channel, and a reputable production company, and they wouldn't dream of recasting anyone for wanting a private space to prepare and change. I've often been told by people in our industry that many producers, in many companies, "test the waters" to see what they can get away with. I told them the opposite of what I'd learned in drama school: the only power we have is the power to say "no." I apologized to the White actress, too. I asked her to rid herself

I told them the opposite of what I'd

learned in drama school:

the only power we have

is the power to say "no."

of her embarrassment; we shouldn't have let that happen, we were sorry.

I was taught, during the whole of my career, "that's just the way it is"; producers negotiating with agents. But when negotiations are done, and in one of the producer's palms sit actors willing to forgo their right to privacy, and in the other, actors who said "no," should they have noticed a racial divide? Should they have seen the slave ship on their hands before we started sailing? If so, what then?

As the producer said, she wasn't racist. I knew that. I've never accused anyone at work of racism, but I've been urged to understand someone "isn't racist" on every job I've acted in since, just by pointing out possible patterns, tendencies. When I agree they aren't racist, but suggest they may be thoughtless on the matter, it doesn't go down very well.

I was taught,

during the whole of my career,

"that's just the way it is."

But if you're not racist, or thoughtless about race, what other thing can you be?

After this, and many other occurrences, I was left unsure of my position on set. I wanted this "other" work I was doing to be acknowledged. After negotiations I was made associate producer.

Chewing Gum aired. My baby had captured an audience: the misfits.

My euphoria from being liked made me so happy. I was suddenly fitting in, I went to press nights and parties, and tried cocaine! I had no job to wake up for in the daytime, so I'd go to more parties in the nighttime! Where I'd have more cocaine. Oh, everybody wanted to be my friend. I'd see old friends, who I couldn't remember because nothing was more important than me, being an actor, on cocaine, with my actor friends.

Every snort masked the misery of losing my motherhood; *Chewing Gum* had graduated, I had nothing to focus on.

I saw my ex. "I hear you're struggling with fame," he said. I sat alone, in silence. A question came to me—five years ago, is this who I imagined I would be? I thought about it, an answer came: "no."

I grabbed someone, I asked for help. But we're not all that lucky.

Sometimes, being a misfit hurts. I can recall rummaging through a gift bag for my first big mainstream award. It contained dry shampoo, tanning lotion and a foundation even Kim Kardashian was too dark for. (A reminder: *this isn't your house.*)

Over time some of us have adopted techniques to turn our feeling of alienation into humor. If you've forgotten the feeling of alienation, how can you laugh at it?

The lack of varied perspective among producers, the lack of misfits producing telly, can have catastrophic consequences. I'll give you an example.

I got another job, after *Chewing Gum*, an acting one, to be filmed for three months, in a place far, far away. I was immediately anxious. I searched online "being a misfit like me in this place far, far away." My anxiety grew. I was told not to worry.

One day, while shooting in this place far, far away, was my birthday. Another misfit and I were carrying groceries home. I started feeling something sharp

Over time some of us have adopted

techniques to turn our feeling of

alienation into humor.

If you've forgotten the feeling of

alienation, how can you laugh at it?

on the back of my ankles. What was that? I turned around to see four men hurling stones at us, their brisk walking turning into light jogging, reloading from the ground whenever their hands emptied of stones. The producers told us to keep calm and carry on, just a few weeks left.

Could this have been managed better? Did it have to be on my birthday? I call that a catastrophic consequence. The producers saw shooting in "that place" as a low-cost haven. They didn't consider the experiences of the Brown and Black cast to meet the morals of their diversity compass, because they didn't think to see things from our point of view.

A White actress in the cast later contacted me. She also felt alienated; people were also pointing and staring at her. She hadn't felt that before and just wanted to talk. I asked her what she thought the root of it was. After some silence she said, "I think it's the color of my hair." I think it was, too.

In the process of writing this essay, I searched online what being "an outsider like her" might be like "in that place." The website for a giant hair company came up first, the specific page: "How to Bleach Hair: The Ideal Technique." And I quote: "Your hair is not really blonde? This is true for 95 percent of all people . . . nature has given only very few of them blonde hair. All but these few women have spirited the natural pigments out of their hair. Among the color treatments, bleaching is still number one on the list."

I wondered why, if 95 percent of us didn't fit something, we would encourage each other to aspire to it, to emulate it?

Chewing Gum was offered a second season. My agent and I thought my being credited an exec producer would be simple. She called to say I would not be made an executive producer. Instead I was given a title I've yet to be told the meaning of, the newly created role that they'd made up just for me—"creative co-producer."

We began shooting.

There was a moment during the shoot . . . what was it? The location? The staging? The writing? Something just didn't feel right. I approached a producer: "Is this good? Why does this feel like shit?" I was visibly anxious. "It doesn't feel very good. Is it good?" I was told by the producer it was "really funny" and "great."

During post-production, it became apparent the channel didn't like the look of that story sequence either. In fact, they despised it. We lost an episode. The channel said that they couldn't give us any more money, however, which forced the umbrella company to make it rain.

I was to write a new episode of *Chewing Gum* that could only take place in one location, with a maximum of two leads and one series regular as cast. It was to be inserted as the new episode four, with episode two becoming episode one, episode this, that, ligaments and limbs of storylines just tossed around to make a version that did look fucked, but was still semi-recognizable as a TV show. They said I didn't have much time as the airdate may not change. I went to write in Zurich. I got thrush, and only when I couldn't afford to buy Canesten it became clear I'd accidentally traveled to the third most expensive city in the world. Another birthday passed out there. I got so hungry I went into McDonald's and asked them for fries; they gave me fries. This is a real-life story.

Somebody gave me something, for nothing in return. I wrote that episode in three days.

I realized the show may look more human if we made the new "ep" episode one, moved a ligament here, swapped the right tit with a testicle and boom, I proposed a version of my child that seemed more "her," which we all agreed worked better.

My exec offered me a production company under his umbrella. He offered this through tears. I'd never seen him cry. I wondered if he really wanted to offer me this, or whether there were feelings of doubt he couldn't quite articulate. I looked the gift horse in the mouth, then used the only power I had, and declined.

Chewing Gum 2 aired. I don't know anything about the online acquisition. I wasn't part of those negotiations, I was just told all rights had been sold to them. Kinda like your dad coming home saying, "This is my new wife, Netanya," and Netanya has no face, that's how impossible transparency seemed. This year, Netanya heard I was pregnant again and wanted to acquire my new unborn for one million dollars, wow.

I've no mortgage, no credit card, no real kids, no car, happy with my bicycle; money's nice, but I prefer transparency. My stories are my babies, I wanna look after them, so I asked to reserve a portion of my parental rights, my copyright. "No, that's not the way it is," said No-Face Netanya. I used the only power I had, and declined.

New writers aren't often made executive producers in the UK. I understand "that's the way it is," that we're not experienced enough to know the budgets, so when and how do we become more experienced? This isn't about me. Luckily, I've learned. This is for the new writers coming after me, so the process of learning isn't harder than it should be. Why not be transparent about the budgets, the figures, the Netanyas? Be more transparent with them about the health and life of the child they're having. Or they're in the dark. As they enlighten you, with TV stories you can't film or write without them, enlighten them; shine a torch on the figures and budgets they can't see.

While researching for this lecture, I offered my first-ever contract to a few writers and some sent theirs in return. It was nice, to be transparent. I spoke to heads of channels, old and new heads of production companies, heads of heads, more heads, loadsa heads. It was interesting, to be transparent, to observe how people ramble, safeguard themselves, then fall silent . . . just before becoming transparent with you. Couldn't get contact information for any board members. Oh well, they probably only make up about 5 percent of our industry anyway.

My research raised questions: I wondered whether someone should investigate how the shows of new writers are budgeted each year, within channels, to look for patterns. It may be that "Business Affairs" have found it easier to get away with spending less on certain shows, sometimes budgeting way below what is commonly held as acceptable. When a budget is lower than standard it leaves production companies saving and scrimping, and that save is often taken out on the writer; for example, the erasure of script editors. I was told while researching for this, "That's the way it is; you wanna put as much money as you can on the screen." Without a healthy writing team, and a great story, what do you have on the screen to inspire misfits? Oh, *Love Island*.

Being more transparent in our industry has led those accused of misconduct to courts. We know this because they're powerful people, who generate clickbait; it makes the papers. Are we protecting those abused by these producers?

Some say our industry is a microcosm of the world. It's a delicate dance, isn't it; the world reflecting us, we, in turn, the world. We have to remember that there are people, outsiders to this industry, being raped by men and women who lack any celebrity status to snatch or public power to dissolve.

I'm going to share two experiences simply and only to discuss their effect on our industry, our house.

I won an award, for writing. At the after-party, a London producer introduced himself to me. I said, "Oh yes, nice to meet you." "Do you know how much I want to fuck you right now?" was his immediate choice of response. I turned from him and went home so quickly I left my plus one. He called, upset. Someone called him a nigger.

It was the same man.

Could my silence have encouraged this producer to push boundaries with women and Black people further? This thought is uncomfortable, but I cannot block it out. I have to face it.

The other experience was a bit more life-changing. I was working overnight in the company's offices; I had an episode due at 7 a.m. I took a break and had a drink with a good friend who was nearby. I emerged into consciousness, typing season two, many hours later. I was lucky. I had a flashback. It turned out I'd been sexually assaulted by strangers. The first people I called after the police, before my own family, were the producers.

How do we operate in this family of television when there is an emergency? Overnight I saw them morph into an anxious team of employers and employees alike; teetering back and forth between the line of knowing what normal human empathy is and not knowing what empathy is at all. When there are police involved, and footage of people carrying your sleeping writer into dangerous places, when cuts are found, when there's blood . . . what is your job?

Could my silence have encouraged

this producer to push boundaries with

women and Black people further?

This thought is uncomfortable, but I

cannot block it out. I have to face it.

Writing felt as though I was cramped in a third of a trailer, a mind overcrowded by flashbacks. I needed to push back the deadline; it was already tight, but just like those actors I wasn't sure how damaging it would be to the company so couldn't ask. I was lucky; someone was transparent with me: "They won't offer you the break," a colleague said. "That's not the way it is. You have to take it."

I asked to push the deadline back and for the channel to be informed as to why. The deadline was pushed back, but the head of comedy never found out why.

Not long after this, in August 2018, I was asked to speak to a room full of people from a creative perspective. At that point in time, I had only made one TV show as a creator/actor and acted in some other roles, and I could only speak from my experience—I was not intending to single anyone out, and made that clear. I also added that this company did send me to a private clinic, a service they offer to staff when in need. The company funded my therapy there until the end of the shoot. I want to stress this: I was not raped within the offices of the company and I have never been raped by anyone at the company.

For survivors of such trauma, therapy's great. And you can get it for free. There are many specialist centers, like The Havens in London, and Survivors Trust, an inclusive service for sexual assault survivors who welcome those who identify as male, trans, nonbinary. Anyone who feels like they're struggling can get free therapy on the NHS. My mum has been a mental health specialist there for a decade; that's why I know. It's good to talk, and engage with someone else, transparently. I believe in treating our minds like we treat cars at inspection—it's probably fine but check in, just in case.

Like any other experience I've found traumatic, it's been therapeutic to write about it, and actively twist a narrative of pain into one of hope, and even humor. And be able to share it with you, as part of a fictional drama on television, because I think transparency helps.

Many of us in the entertainment industry, in this world, are on creaking ladders, climbing, surrounded by noise, stress and nothing real, not even the ladder itself; it can make the future feel bleak and devoid of peace, leaving some feeling isolated to the point of suicide. I think of Anthony Bourdain, who ended his life in June 2018, while shooting a series. I think of Alex Beckett, an actor who ended his life in April 2018, mid a theatre run. I'd worked with him, in that place far away. Is there care for anyone's mind?

Like any other experience I've found

traumatic, it's been therapeutic to

write about it, and actively twist

a narrative of pain into one of

hope, and even humor. And be able

to share it with you, as part of a

fictional drama on television, because

I think transparency helps.

Some find themselves so high their photographs are showcased at prestigious exhibitions in Venice. A Queen was recognized in 2017—Queen Khadija Saye—from the heights of Grenfell Tower. But when the narrative of climbing makes others put profits before people, fitting cheap cladding into their tower blocks, what then? How many other potential artists with stories we want and need have we lost for the sake of financial profit; have we lost to thoughtless education systems, thoughtless nurturing, thoughtlessness? Why are we platforming misfits, heralding them as newly rich successes, while they balance on creaking ladders with little chance of social mobility? I can't help usher them into this house if there are doors within it they can't open. It feels complicit. What I can do is be transparent about my experiences, because transparency helps.

The misfit doesn't climb in pursuit of safety, or profit; she climbs to tell stories. She gets off the ladder and onto the swings; swinging back and forth,

Why are we platforming misfits,
heralding them as newly rich
successes, while they balance on
creaking ladders with little chance
of social mobility? I can't help usher
them into this house if there are
doors within it they can't open. It
feels complicit. What I can do is be
transparent about my experiences,
because transparency helps.

sometimes aggressively, sometimes standing up on the swing, back and forth, in pursuit of only transparency, observing the changes, but wonders if these changes are taking place within a faulty system.

How can we help each other to fix a faulty system? Surely, we can help each other to fix a faulty house.

Being a producer, being head of department, head of the house, being a human, is a noisy job; everything coming at you, from all angles, at all hours. I think it's important to make silence for yourself. Five minutes. To check if you're okay. And interrogate your own morals and beliefs in relation to how you operate. Even if you do think about these things already, why not think a little more, a little deeper?

Accepting we're wrong—that I'm wrong—is hard. I recall a phone call from an exec during season two

The misfit doesn't climb in pursuit

of safety, or profit; she climbs to

tell stories. She gets off the ladder

and onto the swings; swinging back

and forth, sometimes aggressively,

sometimes standing up on the swing,

back and forth, in pursuit of only

transparency, observing the changes,

but wonders if these changes are

taking place within a faulty system.

of *Chewing Gum*. I'd written a part for a Malaysian woman, and one auditionee thought my story was two-dimensional so emailed her feelings. I flailed around like an idiot. "This isn't my department! I'm an artist not a politician! It's finished anyway, I'm not even writing that episode anymore!" I Kat Slatered down the phone.

And in that small gap of silence, I realized that she was right, and rewrote the part; I changed the narrative. And on reflection, I wished I'd just listened. I wished I'd spent more time thinking before I'd acted.

I recall a quote from a book called *Act Accordingly*, by Colin Wright. He said: "There are as many perspectives as there are people." I'll always remember that.

I've decided to embrace as many perspectives as I can, and be brave enough to update my beliefs, and discover I'm not always right. What a brilliant thing, to discover we've been wrong about some things, what a brilliant thing it is to grow. We're all gonna die. Instead of standing here, wishing for the good ol' glory days, about the way life used to be before Mark Zuckerberg graduated, I'm going to try to be my best; to be transparent; and to play whatever part I can to help fix this house. What part will you play?

"There are as many perspectives as

there are people."

Colin Wright

EPILOGUE

The Aftermoth

I write this three years on from the lecture, and I'm still often asked about its aftermath. What its reception felt like. I don't know how the lecture was received by the individual, by the house, by the workforce of my industry or by anyone. I stepped off the podium, went home with my housemate and made a burrito. Had I made sense to them? Had they understood my use of language? Had they connected any of the dots? I truly cannot say. I prefer to investigate what the experience did for me, and I hope that my sharing this might do something for you, too.

While the opportunity to give a lecture might be rare, I hope the lessons I've learned from it are not so. That you close these final pages getting a sense of your life from another perspective and check if your house is in order, to better know who you are, how you're truly doing, and if there's any part of your internal system that is faulty or in need of fixing.

Having the opportunity to speak, to be heard uninterrupted for that length of time (roughly one hour), certainly altered me as a person. It's a privilege; who gets to go that long without the threat of a challenge or retort? Quite wild, really. I reckon it somehow sedated me for a while, but like any drug the effect wears off. I find myself again, standing on swings, looking around my industry, my house—our house—and wondering: *What part can I play? What thing can I contribute or say to help?* Thinking, rethinking and trying to be transparent with myself before I was honest with those in the audience that day perhaps forced me to consider my life more thoroughly, and in turn urged me to be more considerate about the lives of others.

The tales I told myself about the moth—my attempts to try and liken its journey to my own narrative as a human—led me to see the lecture itself, and my giving of it, as a symbol of death. Death to the habit of compartmentalizing pain and avoiding emotions, death to coping so successfully that I put my ability to process life and to grieve in jeopardy.

Speaking can be a terrifying action. Our words—even when spoken from a position so powerless that all that's produced is a moth-like squeak—can be loud enough to wake the house: a house that is often sleeping peacefully and does not want to be disturbed; a house in which perhaps you've found a home; a metaphorical house that keeps your literal house afloat, and respite from the horrible feeling of drowning, drowning with that 95 percent again. My life has changed over the past three years. I understand now why one may avoid anything that jeopardizes acquired safety and sense of belonging. The narrative is clear: "Once upon a time, I was a misfit. How lucky I am to find acceptance, to feel safe here. I mustn't jeopardize that."

Through doing the opposite and squeaking that lecture to the thousands who operated, controlled and benefited from the peacefully sleeping house that is the television industry, I learned that staying silent for fear of losing safety doesn't compare to the feeling of safety I found within myself from choosing to be fearless in my curiosity to question the house, to question the very identity of the house, and from choosing to question myself.

At the same time, I do not discount the fact that there is merit in avoiding the kind of self-scrutiny I encourage here. And that perhaps this invitation for transparency with the self should come with either a caveat or warning label that it doesn't necessarily lead to more happiness. Self-delusion is one of the brain's greatest tools: I believed anosmia was a superpower responsible for the enhancement of my other senses, and clinging to this belief, however false, provided a way for me to cope with loss while avoiding any feelings of panic, confusion and vulnerability.

Since giving the lecture, I have asked myself what it is about moths that bothered me and most of us so much. Why did we kill them while we drew, collected and chased butterflies as children? Why was the moth excluded from this adoration and left to flutter the skies as a commercially unattractive misfit? And what made them so mesmerized by the very thing that often killed them? And what can happen in your life when you comfort or embrace the things that repel you?

When I started writing this book, the necklace of the death's-head hawkmoth sat nestled in my jewelry box. The chain had broken, as do most material things, despite their sentimental value. As I finished writing the words in these pages, I returned to the box to find the necklace was gone. And although my sense of smell is not entirely back, I can just about notice my own body odor, onions make me cry once more and moth-killer spray—the stench, the idea itself—I find to be utterly unbearable.

NOTES

Claire Foy (p. 35): If you don't have Netflix or haven't seen *The Crown*, I'm sorry.

Boots (p. 59): Funnily enough, not a shoe shop, but a pharmacy chain created by a man called John Boot in 1849. For some reason, he wanted his name to be associated with tampons, panty-hose and laxatives till the end of time.

Kat Slater (p. 64): Who is Kat Slater? Double leopard prints, big gold hoop earrings, knee-high boots, dramatic eye shadow and a thick cockney accent, ends a conversation by slamming a door in your face . . . you get the picture. The BBC originally announced her arrival to *EastEnders* by describing her as: "a bit of a floozy," "fiery," "a bitch" and "feisty."

A note on moths

Thank you to the Angela Marmont Centre for UK Biodiversity at the Natural History Museum for their help with lepidopterology facts from around the world.

ACKNOWLEDGMENTS

Thank you:

Marisa Cudjoe

Trecia Gyamfuah

Nichaela Fraser

Shakira Prescod

Kate Barlow

Amy

Bianca Kwarteng

Joanna Uwudie

Jenine Rennie

Rochelle Emmanuel

Maame Adjekum

Celestina Kwegan

Ashley Davies

Piers Wenger

Ian Mill and Beth Clayden

Joel Borquaye

Isaac Borquaye

Dad

Samuel Abeiku Williams

ACKNOWLEDGMENTS

Ché Walker

Danny McGrath

Arinzé Kene

Inua Ellams

Olisa Odele

Kadiff Kirwan

Jessica Boyd

Sadie Williams

Veniece Forde

Rachel 'Okay' Ohene-Kodua

Deborah Copaken

To those who helped for nothing in return

About the Author

Michaela Coel is the creator of the hit TV shows *I May Destroy You* and *Chewing Gum*. She has won awards from BAFTA, the Royal Television Society, the Broadcasting Press Guild and the NAACP for her acting, screenwriting and directing. In 2020, she was included in *Time* magazine's 100 Most Influential People and British *Vogue*'s 2020 Most Influential Women lists. *Misfits* is her first book.